Shades Drawn Back

Nana Kay

Resonant Voice
Collection

Table of Contents

I would like to thank my family, friends, and readers for all of the help and support for making this collection a reality.

This book is dedicated to the restless souls with voices the world continuously strives to shut away. May they all find the fire to push forward with their own avenue to express all they have to say.

Preface

Being that this is my first book publication, I've spent a number of days contemplating what to write to you—the person who decided to take the chance to read this. I've pondered over what words I could convey without sounding like a cliché or the constant marketing pushed out to us each day. Honestly, I don't have a reason why you should read this, no more than I have a reason as to why you should choose to have an experience. If you're looking for a justification from me to measure if reading this book is worth your time...you picked up the wrong pages.

I write about the human heart for what it is and what it will be should we continue to abuse ourselves and one another while turning a blind eye. These are truths many people DON'T want to hear—truths oftentimes hidden behind the glamour we paint or the fears we amplify. You may not want to think about those truths yourself, and that's okay. There's a saying many of us know all too well... "ignorance is bliss," and it truly can be. It can make the world into a much simpler place. Sometimes, I wish I could return there, but growing to understand how this world operates, I realize I can't turn away. Unfortunately, such insight can slowly make a person like me, who tends to spend a lot of time in her thoughts, lose her sanity. Therefore, I write as a way of finding my path back to bliss, even if it is for but a moment. The results are words etched with elements of my spirit, woven into a message.

If you do choose to continue, thank you. Maybe you're like me...continually connecting the dots of this wild journey called life. However, understand that, like me, you may also be leaving bliss behind, even if only temporarily. Then again, that is life—challenging the known and facing the unfamiliar.

From my tears, emerged my spears
—words I take with me, into battle.

Hidden Agenda

Hate comes in all shapes and forms,
But the worst, by far, is the hate
Concealed well by trendy societal norms

Inclusion is pushed as the sole mission,
Yet, being part of "the inner club"
Comes with an unspoken condition

Who says agree to everything that's said,
Because using a platform to be heard,
You can't always look to please instead

Forced to conform beyond sense of self,
Loss of individuality, slave to social identity,
Becomes the wallet for commercial wealth

What serves as an ideal tool for profit
Is the hatred of one towards another,
Painted as the "us versus them" composite

Let's begin to ask what's to be gained
Shaming people for parts we don't like,
When we ourselves, are also stained

It's a matter of time before we're estranged
From a future of true understanding,
Forever lost, from actual change

What We've Become

We don't talk, we fight,
Throwing emotional might,
We turn flowers to fences
And set gardens alight

We're about the "one-up" game,
Trashing tact or tame,
"Don't care who you are,
You just remember my name"

With weapons in hand,
We draw lines in the sand,
Before anything's aired,
You're now on enemy land

We pay forward our hate
With rising interest rate,
Forgetting it's taxed
By our karma's due date

Decked out with complexes
And our nonsensical vexes,
We lend credence to reason
When feeding ego flexes

It's "come at me, I'm ready,"
Whether it's heavy or petty,
Casting away all the wisdom
Meant to keep us, steady...

Well, what do you expect
From how little we reflect,
We celebrate the ruthless,
Holding them high in respect

We've become a cold culture
Of the ever-preying vulture,
Looking down from our perch
At each carcass to pick and torture

What have we become?

Hypocrisy

We speak on diversity,
But spit out our spite,
As we brand who's our enemy,
Among the neighbors we fight

Our social, our charity,
To give self to the world,
But selfless acts to popularity,
Enslave us to the digital word

In a growing connectivity
That's detached from the sanity

We're conformed to a society,
Removed from morality

Very soon one's identity
Is torn down by the majority

And what's left becomes
A human philosophy,
Bound in our hypocrisy

For lives we leave behind,
Buried with all our praise,
When they lived, we declined
To give them our better ways

We act out our difference,
Boldly showing our truth,
Yet we're laughed by the world
When freely living our youth

Being crushed by the strain,
We're made numb to the pain

Our prayers and hopes grow faint
To the cruel realities we paint

Soon we're filled with regret,
Within the heart we forget

And what's left becomes
A human philosophy,
Bound in our hypocrisy

Cracked is the reality,
The ideal we all yearned,
But even more disturbing
Is finding this all is learned

We revel in constitution
Built on our disillusion,
Just to be leveled by institution,
Upheld by our confusion

Was there ever a plan,
Beyond the division of man

We broke down bonds of trust,
And replaced it with blood lust

What creed did we sign,
If our choices came to define

What's now left,
Is a human philosophy,
Bound in our hypocrisy

First, we walk a path with ourselves
As our only devoted company,
Devoid of outside praise,
As we fumble forward, clumsily

We look for warm validations
Within the nooks of society,
Ignoring our inner voice,
We give in to our anxiety

Funny, we become a person
People want to know,
Only when we've got
Something flashy to show

Through trial and error
We soon find who is true,
But the end result, sadly,
Might yield less than few

With experienced eyes
We traverse the world,
Learning to adapt beyond
What's simply observed

We soon carve our path
By laying our doubt aside,
Remembering once more,
Our inner voice inside

We eventually move forward,
Building something of our own,
Finding meaning in our journey,
And feeling a little less alone

I'll choose no side.
I mission my petition
For my choice to decide.
My place, in this space
Is one, that I run,
Within my own mind.

Why must it be
Us versus them,
On the offense
To condemn,
The other with pride?

Can we inspire
The youth,
To rise
To their truth,
When hearts are denied?

People are now read,
Before anything's said,
Outright...

What is freedom worth,
Walking this earth,
Zombified...?

We come to appropriate, what we don't appreciate.
No wonder we become irate
when something once considered innate,
is now some historical find, or a newly discovered trait.
Devoid of ownership, we take,
withdrawn from humility, we claim,
tagging what we imitate—others' cultural state
—by an empty name. All this, to feed and appease
a world that gravitates, towards
the trendy images we paint
with harsh, overlaying patterns across
what was already regarded as great,
now repackaged as novelty.
With no context given, nor any price paid,
we strip away the core essence—the meaning
—lost in a trade, substituted for clout presence.
Imagine... throwing shade, would have dealt
a lesser injury, but this is what breeds today's hate
—exploitation—an act we drive to perpetuate,
as a means towards self-elation,
in a world ruled by click bait.

In a world of plenty,
Seen small by those
With hearts so empty,
Seeking to covet all
By means of any

Looking only to claim
Power over another,
To establish a name
That lives on forever
In the conqueror game

You subjugate a nation,
Erase their history
To elevate your station,
Only to apologize, well after,
In a false revelation

You steal all their jewels,
Their riches, raid
And plunder their tools,
And to add insult to injury,
You label their people, fools

Guess those in power
Make up all the rules,
Watching from their tower,
They look down on others
As only prey, to devour

Once Ours, Now Theirs

We continue to auction
The world all our stuff,
But haven't we been
Colonized far enough?

We give them rights
To own our fertile land,
Then have our own
People buy dry sand

A future can't be gleaned
By growing singular greed,
When too blind to see
Lasting damage to our seed

What do we do
When we've sold it all?
Will we have any nations
To belong to, at all?

Fairytales make ruling queens evil,
Textbooks show us the madness of kings,
And yet, stories of such corrupted people
Began from stained beginnings

Visuals of power and status
Are not depicted as images of meek,
So rejecting benevolence for malice,
Is revered as what a ruler must seek

Within a court, you eat or be eaten
Inside a fortified prison of stone,
If you survive, without a spirit left beaten,
You're moved to seek out a seat of your own

Inheritance gets slimmer to gain
In lieu of a line of succession,
So now you ponder how to obtain
Position—an aim, which becomes obsession

You play everyone like chess pieces
To achieve an influence you can claim,
Because the lessons that history teaches
Has record of such legends, by name

When you finally make it to the top
To seize your victory upon the throne,
You realize, your carnage can never stop,
If you are to keep such rewards, for your own

True Consent

Consent is not a pass
To get what you want to get,
It's a mutual understanding,
Not devoid of its respect

The first concrete step
Begins with one's permission,
That's only one part of the process,
Not the final decision

It can be withdrawn
At any point of time, once given,
And the act of doing so
Should not be considered forbidden

Why can something so simple
Be beyond comprehension,
It's not rocket science we're teaching,
It's basic human affection

Valued

Can a heaven exist,
In a place called hell,
If a price placed on life,
Is but an easy sell?

What comes to determine
The worth we each bring,
If the judge isn't judged
By the very same thing.

When you bathe in infamy
And you come to tell it,
They'll put a price tag
On you, and sell it.

And when you're nameless
You'll come to wear it,
Parading around as
Their mascot parrot.

Through generations,
The sparks diminish,
Replaced by a cheap,
Mimic glamour finish.

What if it were to be said
That what lasts on earth,
Are products made on
Supply chains of rebirth.

When the day of reckoning
Cycles back around,
Will all be laid bare,
Our roots naked, above ground?

Money Is Funny

When left to the single mom
Hustling to bring her family calm,
Yeah, it's not all about money

When drugs are like sweet honey
To the whacked-out junkie,
Tell me, it's not all about money

When things seem less sunny
Cause you're struggling in pain,
Watching the world around you
Using your suffering to entertain

It may not be all about money,
But we all bleed for green to gain

It's money that always runs the game

When the streets turn bloody
Living in slums of the born unlucky,
Is it really not all about money?

You're working hard to study,
When your competitor is your buddy,
How can it be all about money?

When clear waters turn murky,
And fresh lakes become so unclear,
We wait for its sands to settle,
Hoping for the aquatic life to appear

It may not be all about money,
But we all pray for it out of fear

It's a craving itch to have money near

When you're left alone, cast aside,
Just a prop taken along for the ride,
Sure, it may not be status-tied

When you put your health on hold
To prioritize a piling billing load,
Surely, it's not the lack of mining gold

When you're a target of envy
From what people outwardly see,
Maybe it's not linked to dollar-popularity

When you can't live without limits
Without avoiding inward grimace,
Maybe it's not your account's lacking digits

A lot of life revolves around money,
But you want to know what's quite funny
We proudly say, "it's not for me"

But as you can see...it's all about money

Game, Set, and Match

Did you really expect
Large corporations to value respect,
Banks collect your net worth,
Only to cash out on a check

Ads tailored for us to begin
Our ultimate passion win,
With capital venture spin,
—A dreamscape painted, out of gambler's sin

Funding our own grassroots startup,
Is the new 21st century pin-up,
A symbol of vanity to hoist up
Our "overnight" fame jump

Today, it's about a final percentage,
Between you and what you can leverage,
We're a slave to the markup
Within a monopolized marriage

While we push on with our pursuits
Beyond limitations and absolutes,
We have a new hamster wheel to run on
Just to continually produce

We simply come to concede
To the sacrifices we bleed,
In hopes it's not empty promise
As we each climb up to succeed

We seek a victory to the game,
But will it be ours or theirs to proclaim,
Who'll be the ones that will reap
All the possible rewards in this game

Veiled Transparency

Companies constantly seem,
To want their ads
Scrubbed family-clean,
If only the same were to be seen,
For ingredients their labs
Continually glean

"Going green" is their trend,
Much so they are willing
To frame that up and pretend,
That poor practices they defend,
Are not in line with the rules
And guidelines they bend

They know a society made drunk,
Is much easier
To plump up with junk,
Thinking we got all the luck
With deals, stiffing us
Against the value of a buck

But will we be privy to know
The extent of where
All this will go,
I wish standards weren't so low,
And all this performance
Wasn't only for show

Another trip to the doctor
While trying to proctor your condition,
You hope to get care and attention,
But end up with only a prescription

You're explaining what you're feeling,
But for healing, you're ultimately told,
That you're simply over-thinking,
"It's not serious, but just a small cold"

In your mind, there's silent unrest,
Pain in the chest, war in the body,
But urging a lab test to be done,
Seems like you're trying to lobby

Not enough time to go over
All of your bodily symptoms,
By the next visit, more is added
To the list of microbic victims

You have to play like the lottery,
Just to afford a second, or third opinion,
By the time one is found,
You're now back at the very beginning

Conditioned to seek a quick fix—
A mixture of temporary solution,
Written up in big formulas
And distributed as mere substitution

But the hard truth is, it's a system,
A cut-and-dry model business service,
With sickness, the commodity,
Funneled by big pharma and insurance

Eventually the alarms start to sound,
With the room now spinning,
You're soon bound for the ER,
Diagnosed with a lifeline, thinning...

Cash Cow, Piggy Bank

The cow eats whole earth,
The pig feasts on scrap slops,
But fresh greens to the pig,
Somehow never stops...

Calls to a community come collect,
Built on sheer hopes of mutual respect,
But loyalty, you should not expect,
Since the context of one's character,
Is always considered most suspect

Few words from unguarded lips,
Could gain you a few ego trips,
Within your social's addictive grips,
But humbled you'll soon become,
When favor takes its sharp dips

Being bombarded by societal hits,
Can be deadlier than a reaper's kiss,
When placed on the naughty list,
Know that actions aren't erased,
Even midst an apology, they still exist

A trust you may look to take,
Could land you burned at the stake,
Sooner than any PR story you can make,
There will always be a price placed
On top of every human mistake

Beloved Titles

We worship titles,
Exalting them up as our idols,
While dancing around our society's
Rapidly draining vitals.

Does one need a throne,
In order to be known?
When did singular roles,
Determine the value we own?

If only the same could be said
About one's character instead.
What will become its worth
In the future ahead?

Life In Boxes

Slaves continually hope to live past
An era which binds them to their caste,
They grasp hairs of an elusive freedom,
Praying for salvation, unbound to a mausoleum.

A Worker bee—backbone of the hierarchy—
Is no longer slave ousted by society,
But they too look to become free,
Thinking they paid in full their fee.

On to the elites, who now have their seats
At the table, finally finding their peace,
But loss of it all, shackles them to their fears,
To leave such a life behind, in the rears...

Sitting on the top of the social crop,
Is a star on the tree—the most coveted prop—
Housing the decorated noteworthy royal,
Surrounded by subjects, only bought loyal.

What does it truly mean to become free,
If this system has defined our history.
Always designated a box of where to reside,
Can grass really grow greener, on the other side...?

Social pop cults are never
Considered heathen,
Though they're devoid
Of all rhyme or reason.
That's how strong emotion
Drives mass believing,
In a herd, a simple trend
Can be slay of the season.

A cult without borders,
Is rarely divided by orders,
But you're nonetheless shamed
From becoming transformers.
Why not be encouraged
To be today's daring explorers?
Let's stop the baseless tortures
Of type-casting people
Into and out of certain cultures.

Beasts We Create

At times, it takes flesh stripped bare,
Or mind toyed around without care,
Pieces of self, scattered beyond repair,
In a cold world requiring you to fare

Weighing down a spirit, once light,
Its will, beaten and suffocated tight,
Left to crumble beneath sheer fright
Of shadows closing in on one's plight

Leaving only an animal in our wake,
That turns to survival, midst heartache,
Possessed by desire and purpose to take,
No longer blessed to sleep, nor to break

Soon the carnage becomes too great,
Destruction to burst forth with hate,
Unable to turn back to a brighter fate,
And reverse the beast, we create

Zombies

Zombies exist, starting
As a disease in the heart,
A plague in which the core,
Once whole, slowly withers apart

Zombies exist, within
Those denied worthy praise,
Those harbored away from self,
And those society failed to raise

Zombies exist, as sprouts
Of society's budding youth
Are plucked from their Eden,
Kept away from living their truth

Zombies exist, growing
In number with every cry,
New brains cultivated for harvest
Wandering purpose, their why

Zombies exist, in vain
They seek a life worth more,
But all the while dead
To what their life is lived for

Starting within, as sprouts
Growing in vain, zombies exist...

Buried Composites

Our symbol is red, white and blue
Yet many ask "what color are you?"
What is it really that we hold true,
Shouldn't values be our only hue
Among the many, instead of the few?

However, don't try profiling this
As me speaking on nationalistic bliss,
This is not meant for you to dismiss
Lived moments of those whom you diss,
Or else, the message will surely be missed

Time has come to reveal the truths
Of rotting bodies under pristine roofs,
The public has now seen the proof
That today's justice is political spoof,
Seeking a permit to cripple its youth

Being able to walk in others' shoes
Is not the social media filter you use,
Nor your political agenda to ruse
And gather up the minions you choose
As you step up to collect your dues

Do better, and choose to be more
Than whatever society clamors for,
Doing right is no thing of lore,
Let us believe that at our core,
Gold can still be mined from our ore

Common Ground

The sweet honey harvested
From flowering buds of May,
Arise from tended soils,
Raised from fires of "us" and "they"

Twisted tendrils deep rooted,
Are not simply a product of birth,
But rather they're cultivated within
The societal vegetation of our worth

People are truly seen in the right
From actions viewed from their sight.
When painted different in another light,
They fall from grace at anointed height.

When does action become treachery,
If definition changes with each century.
In a holy reverie, we gown depravity,
Slipping ever closer into moral jeopardy.

Using fear of tyranny to lead the crusade,
Rallying loyal populous, we can persuade.
Splitting societal hairs with righteous tirade,
We nail to the cross traitors we can parade.

Biases root our communal barricade,
That bloom into the prideful accolade.
Like flies to trash, we blindly aggregate
Around what society loves to fabricate,

And at the center stands a puppeteer magistrate.

Casting Judgment

They want someone to
Point at and blame,
To prop up while
Dragging their name,
A bright example
To boycott and defame,
A swift drive-by to
Out them from the game

What becomes the goal,
Berating actions of figures
You don't even know,
When you still purchase
Tickets to their success show,
Can you really say you're fit
To deal first and final blow,
You say they're incapable of change,
Unwilling to develop and grow,
So then say you're without sin,
With a stone in hand, ready to throw

In-Between The Lies

Taking a much closer inspection
Will reveal deep rumblings of insurrection
From a society unhinged and unwoven,
Spilling forth with many promises, left broken.

It's now time to gather ourselves around
To learn of cold truths, soon to be unbound
By warmth of charm and the allure of spell
—Tales our world always loves to tell.

We learn of humanity's story
Through visages of men, slave to glory,
But is his-story the only one to stand
While there's others yet to be written by hand?

A hearty, one-sided narration,
Made concrete with divine indoctrination,
Serves to embolden legacies of a nation
Into further pomp and self-justification.

Our rites to conquest began the assault
On lands and territories dressed up with fault
By our forces of creed, led by sinister hands,
Severing people from customs through social bans.

Through inflated images of altruism,
Which both fulfill and excuse our narcissism,
We outwardly deny our role of self
From acts we call, "spreading the wealth."

We refuse to deny the value of a dollar,
Giving money more worth than that of our honor,
We're tripping to climb over one another,
Killing, just to make it out, and back into the gutter.

When we come together to sing out our praises,
It's all cameras, big smiles, and fond gazes,
But blood soon rolls down each of our backs,
Following calculated back-stabbed attacks.

Perhaps today's kindness only became trendy
Because in practice, we'd sooner turn to envy.
We put on a face to make ourselves feel better,
Choosing to hide behind disdain and displeasure.

We relish in discussing living with tolerance,
Yet, still want a society that's quite homogenous,
Different minds can no longer make their sound
When we've buried them deep, six-feet underground.

We still search for our signs and miracles
Through dry sermons and showy spirituals,
Blind to blessings we have so near,
Choosing to instead place more faith in our fear.

Many hearts remain more closed than open
As words of love to be shared are left unspoken,
Every civilization began with a declaration,
Yet we'd rather bury the power of a conversation.

I hope the spirit of truth is what prevails
But to pursue it means uncorrupting the details.
It's not a chore, nor a job...but a matter of choice,
Not a tweet to be read, but should be said, in one voice.

Behind The White Picket Fence

You try to call us out in vain,
Despite us keeping grounded,
You're driven to brand us, "insane"

Hate and fire are your campaign,
Your words prove unfounded,
Sacrilegious, with no restrain

Using God's name, you proclaim
That we're the spawns of Eve,
Bearing the cursed mark of Cain

Your verses become your stain,
For sin is the virus we all carry,
Far from immune to the strain

Stripping away all matter of pretense,
We can finally be free to strive
For each other's mutual reverence

But in a single last-ditch defense,
You put up your walls,
Peering behind a white picket fence

Hurling curses of intolerance,
Behind comforts of self-infliction,
Afforded by rooted ignorance...

Moral Dichotomy

Those of us with eyes, don't seek
To lift those who weep,
Yet leap at the chance
To make fleeting smiles weak

At times, it's a promise said,
When it's not a vow to keep,
From our lips, even a lie
Can be as nectar, tasting as sweet

Our mutual harvests are bled
So today, we bear the feat,
Until the time later comes
To glean from barren, cold peat

We admonish abundance,
But on grandeur we eat,
Even as anguished voices
Are laid down at our feet

Even as we see bodies bleeding
Away into pools of red sea,
We press on with conquest
And greed, veiled as our piety

Words and actions have their dance
Moving in moral dichotomy,
Two faces of the same coin
Whirling on, for all eternity

Etched

Blood is thicker than water, they say,
But so too is the mud we all return to one day.
When all that blood finally drains away—swallowed
by the earth—what will remain in the dirt,
beyond the bones and clay? Perhaps, there lies invisible
woven threads of bonds continuing to stretch.
Over lifetimes, may they remain tethered—
a memento beyond body—in time, forever etched.

Are the Greats, only mere martyrs,
Of a time long gone by?
Where do we pry legend from mortal—
Oh, how these lives are now weighted,
Made gold marble, well after they die!
But in that glow, we forgot that their humanity
Was something we were once driven to deny.
We erased their mothers, fathers and families,
Stealing away their peace to freely cry,
While they were reminded of the moment
They never got, to extend a final goodbye.

For the lives that were once
Degraded, berated and beaten for no crime,
We were the Peters who thrice turned away
From the Son at the most critical time.
Their essence, we stripped away
When we recited their speeches, line by line.
Even now, they're words are re-written,
Remolded to fit within our own design.

And yet...somehow their spirit thrives

Somewhere, within our crippling pains,
In the recollections of our relished joys,
In moments of our losses and gains.
Though we tore down their very being,
Miraculously, their humanity remains...

When we resurrect these unforgotten figures,
Let's carry them in our darkness and our light
Midst our flaws, our dreams, and our purpose
For those are the reasons we choose to fight.

Remember, those were their reasons too...

The Fight

With a desire to make things right,
We hold on to so much hurt, for no justice tonight.
Today's heavy souls were once light;
In this dark hour we ask ourselves, how can we fight?
Against the waves of shifting plight,
With fists clenched so tight, how can we fight?

Some throw rocks with anger and spite
Using all their mustered might,
While others recite stirring words to excite.

For me, I simply open up a page, and I write.

If we are to fight, may it be for tomorrow's bright.
Rather than just ignite cities,
May we set our own souls alight,
Driving a war-torn world to unite,

And raising a future up, to a new height.

Music and spoken word were big inspirations for many of the poetry pieces in "Shades Drawn Back," much so I decided to combine both into video representations for a few of my poems. To see those videos, use the QR code below and you'll be taken to one of my YouTube playlists titled, Full-Length Poetry. Go, and have an experience...

About the Author

The woman behind the Nana Kay pseudonym is a published writer who began her poetry journey at 18 years old, with her first publication making it into a nationally-recognized magazine. Since that time, she's continued to dedicate herself to creative writing and storytelling through poetry, prose, and visual content creation. Holding a B.A. in Psychology, she possesses a deep fascination in the human mind and heart in addition to their impacts on different forms of identity.

With hopes to inspire different ways of exploring the spirit of voice, she desires to surface critical conversations between perceptions and realities of the human experience. Nana Kay draws inspiration from current events, traditional and nontraditional literature, music, performance art, and spirituality. She currently resides in the Chicagoland area with her family.

You can follow Nana Kay on:

- Instagram @resonant.voice
- TikTok @resonant.voice
- YouTube @resonantvoicecollection

Don't miss out!

Visit the website below and you can sign up to receive emails whenever Nana Kay publishes a new book. There's no charge and no obligation.

https://books2read.com/r/B-A-KRQV-VPNCC